IDEAL
Possibility

IDEAL
Possibility

Claudia Zamora

Ideal Possibility

Author:
Claudia Zamora

ISBN-13:
978-1-4783-8523-3
Second Edition: August 7, 2012
CreateSpace

978-1-4269-4624-0
First Edition: November 15, 2010
Trafford Publishing

Contact:
www.claudiazamora.net

To the reason for my existence:
Claudia Camilla,
Melissa, Pablo & Axel

"The reality we live
is what we imagine."

Contents

Vibration

> "*Nothing is immobile; everything moves;*
> *everything vibrates.*"
>
> —HERMES TRIMEGISTO

This principle, envisaged over three thousand years ago, embodies the truth of what we are and of the world that surrounds us. It explains the differences between the various manifestations of living matter —physical forces, the mind and even the spirit— all of which are merely the result of diverse vibratory states.

From the Almighty, which is pure spirit, to the coarsest form of matter, everything is in constant vibration.

Everything moves.

Vibrations are defined as the oscillating movement that a particle makes around a fixed point.

One of the most famous formulas that Albert Einstein originated is $E=mc^2$. Physically, we are energy, and everything that surrounds us is formed by energy. We are all part of a great energy field.

Everything that we perceive as solid and separate is a different way of perceiving our vital energy, which is common to all things in the universe.

Energy vibrates at different velocities, thus it displays different qualities, some are more subtle and others are denser.

Thoughts are a relatively subtle and light form of energy; hence they can change rapidly and easily.

Matter is a denser and more compacted form of energy, therefore it is slower to move and change.

Within matter there also are great variations.

We can say that the human body is relatively subtle and changes rapidly, being affected by many factors and variations.

A stone is a much denser, slowly changeable form of material, and nothing affects it easily. Yet, with its heavy cosmology, the stone also varies and changes in accordance with the energy that affects it.

For example, water is able to affect a stone's energy and shape.

All forms of energy are interrelated and are able to affect one another.

Matter and energy are only the result of different vibratory states.

The spirit is at a more elevated vibratory polar extreme and matter is at a denser vibratory polar extreme.

In between both extremes, our thoughts, emotions, desires, and impulses are vibratory states of intermediate frequencies.

Our physical body is a set of systems that vibrate in the same frequency.

When we enjoy good health, our biological systems are dancing in perfect harmony.

They vibrate in tune.

In the realm of our personal life, everything revolves around vibration; if we are happy, it is due to positive vibration, whereas sadness is a negative vibration.

Every person possesses their own mental wave length, in accordance with the vibratory frequency of their intelligence; the shorter the mental wave, the more intelligent the person will be and vice versa.

Our behavioral habits, emotional states, habitual thoughts, and spiritual and moral standards can determine the goodness or inconvenience of our vibratory states which, in turn, decisively influence and impact our daily life.

Positive or negative vibrations tend to build up inside of us and, at a certain point in time; some trigger causes the accumulation to burst, thus causing highly charged and emotional events to occur.

A musical note is a tone, a pitch or frequency. When this

frequency is doubled produces a higher pitched note in its frequency, we call it an "octave".

Octaves infinitely sound above and below our musical scale.

By some strange coincidence, there are fifty octaves in a tone of one per second - the lowest frequency of the human heart- beat, and to the frequency of visible light.

A tone or beat is barely a few octaves lower than what we hear as music, while light and color are dozens of octaves above music.

A chord is two notes or tones occurring simultaneously.

All chords produce their own unique sound because when we play two notes together, a third note or tone is also heard.

This third tone is not inherent to either of the two notes, but is created as a synergetic consequence of their unification in our brain.

The tones within the notes are the interaction of a series of harmonics.

The human brain can perceive the presence of intermediate subliminal notes and; follow the pattern and its interactions beyond the sound that allows it.

The different waves that correspond to the different fractions of sound are what we call harmonics, which can intercept any vibratory event including atomic vibration.

The wave interactions that occur in a musical chord are the same interactions that govern how molecules attract or repel each other, how ocean waves successively follow each other and in what gravitational orbits the planets revolve in.

The musical scale is not a mere accident..

It is the natural consequence of the pure mathematics that permeates all of nature.

We can say that we have discovered it, more than we have invented it.

Pythagoras asserted that mathematics demonstrated the exact method by which goodness was established and maintained in the universe.

Numbers precede harmony, being the immutable law that governs all harmonic proportions.

This is one of the reasons why music can be considered as the true universal language.

Music is vibratory physics and mathematics that is perceived almost as a language is sensed by the ear and brain or its combination.

Great philosophers have said that harmony is an immediate prerequisite to beauty, since beauty is the result of a harmonious combination of different components.

Quantum Physics teaches us that our physical body is continuously exchanging atoms with the environment.

When we inhale we take in the atoms of the environment and when we exhale we give back the atoms of our own physical body.

Literally, when we enter into a location, we begin to absorb part of it. This is the reason why some places fill us with positive energy or to the contrary.

Natural settings such as beaches, mountains, forests, lakes and the like are charged with positive vibrations.

When we remain there, our physical body is renewed with high quality vibratory atoms.

We automatically feel a general state of well-being when we are in contact with these high vibratory locations.

Oppositely, when we have tarried for a certain amount of time in a place that has low or negative vibrations, we feel contaminated.

Such is the case with people who work in hospitals and interact with patients suffering from health conditions and painful diseases.

Even though they adopt a positive attitude every day, the very same energy of that environment pervaded with pain and concern, becomes contagious and many times they need a change of environment or temporary isolation to release the contaminated vibratory energy stored within their auras.

Music neutralizes contaminated energies.

Pythagoras asserted there was a "musical medicine" that healed the body, mind and spirit, and many people and places neutralize their vibratory states through functional music.

One of the most interesting discoveries of quantum physics is that the results of any experiment will largely depend on the level of expectations of the researcher.

What causes atoms to group together and produce changes in our bodies is the idea or thought that governs our mind.

It was formerly believed that if two people carry out the same trial, with identical elements and measurements, they would achieve the same outcome.

Today we know that atoms gather together according to their compatibility and respond to the expectations of the observer.

This is the reason why a person is able to prepare a very delicious meal that no one else can reproduce; because even though we may carefully follow all the recipe instructions and use the same ingredients, the result will never be exactly the same.

The outcome always depends on the expectations of the observer and his personal interest in the experiment.

We can easily infer from this that the tastiest meal is the one that contains love as the main ingredient.

In this manner, everyone is able to surround themselves with the people and places that are vibrating at the same compatible frequency with theirs.

It is impossible to attract situations or objects with high vibration if one is at a lower vibration level.

Depression, anguish, fear, disease and negative emotions cause us to vibrate at a lower level where we cannot even envision solutions to our problems.

Nothing flows and everything is energetically stagnant

within that vibratory level.

Density and negativity from the environment is breathed in.

The highest vibratory level corresponds to illumination, peace and complete, perfect love.

Here exist no problems, fears or diseases.

When one vibrates at this level, whatever he thinks is manifested immediately.

There is complete and absolute awareness of our personal power and we generally use it to serve humanity.

When we improve upon our personal vibration, we reciprocally improve upon the vibration of everyone around us.

Like energies attract each other.

This means that when our personal vibration is extremely low, problems will arise.

We should then endeavor to attract more positive situations and people to our lives to enhance the vibratory frequency that surrounds us, and thus raise ours, in order to help us vibrate in happiness.

Love is the highest vibratory level that we can reach.

Thanks to Love we can move, relate to others, heal and develop ourselves.

Love surpasses our physical reality and it is an unconditional soul experience that ebbs and flows throughout life.

The Almighty is supreme love.

Even so, many people do not permit love's vibration to

enter into their lives for fear of commitment to these sensations, intentions, desires and ambitions.

But love's energy is what makes our purpose possible.

It has the power to create, motivate, inspire, heal, and fill us with dynamism.

When we do not have sufficient motivation to live a purposeful life, we should ask ourselves:

- o How is love's energy flowing in my life?
- o What am I doing to increase the vibration of love's energy?

Love is neither conditional nor limited to a daily dose.

And contrary to what we think, love's energy flows throughout all the far reaches of our planet and to every living thing.

By just looking around us, we can see that all of creation vibrates in this frequency of infinite love.

We need to recharge our vibration level with the powerful energy of unconditional love.

When we increase this energy, we are letting all the positive things that vibrate in this frequency to come to us.

Prosperity and abundance are seeds of goodness in the universe of love.

The simplicity of love amazes us with its strength.

It heals all frustrations and it is a source of real transforming power in our lives.

It is a unifying force.

When we vibrate with love's energy, we feel connected to something or someone.

The kinds of actions that are derived from this energy and contribute to growth are validation, acknowledgement, admiration, appreciation, and thankfulness to something or someone.

When we perform some or all of these actions, we are elevating the love energy in the relationship we have with ourselves, with others, and the ambience around us.

Our plants and flowers receive that positive or negative vibratory charge.

Have you ever noticed how many times a flower instantly withers when a negative person is nearby?

At the same time, we can observe that our plants grow constantly, radiant and fragrant, when our vibration level is positive and loving.

Love transforms everything.

Love *can do anything.*

2

Rhythm

> *"Everything ebbs and flows; everything advances and retreats; all things rise and fall; everything swings like a pendulum, its measured movement to the right is the same as its movement to the left; the Rhythm is the compensation."*

In the infinite myriad of activities that govern the existence of all living things, rhythm is manifested.

We observe rhythm in geophysical phenomena such as ocean tides, the solar day, lunar month and seasonal changes.

It is a controlled flow of sound and visual movement, typically generated by the ordering of different elements in each unique environment.

Rhythm is manifested between the two poles of the Almighty.

However, this does not mean that the rhythmic oscillation reaches each pole's extreme, for this rarely happens; in the majority of cases, it is very difficult to establish the extreme of each opposite pole.

But oscillation first swings to one pole and then to the other.

There is always oscillation, an advance and a retreat, a rise and a fall manifesting itself in all the things and phenomena of the universe.

We see the rhythm in the suns, worlds, minds, energy, spirit, matter, animals and plants.

We see it in the life history of all things, in the rise and fall of nations, that is to say, this principle is at work at all levels and planes.

In music, we observe that it is the musical rhythm that gives music its frequency and provides its basic rhythm and definition.

Rhythm has a lot to do with defining the beat; the kind of beat that, in turn, defines the accentuated emphasis and the musical notes which compose it.

By putting together the emphases, musical notes and beat defined by the rhythm, the melody materializes.

In other words, the rhythm is based on and supported by the musical accents that give it structure.

The melody gives form and shape to all of this.

In written prose, the rhythmic impulse determines the balance of the sentences and disposition of the words.

Rhythm is a basic feature of poetry, which determines its

structure by the well-planned succession of long and short syllables.

Rhyme also contributes to the rhythmic effect.

In the visual arts, objects and figures are placed in juxtaposition to each other in order to create a rhythmic composition.

The concept of rhythm is suggestive of music, melody, pulsation, and beat, and in this manner, all of existence conducts itself each day.

The universe impacts and affects the human organism, every living thing, and vice versa; that is why there are certain times to eat, work and rest which are the most optimal for maintaining balance and health.

Life has its rhythm which we can observe in our daily environment.

At dawn, it seems as if an orchestra conductor moves his baton and alerts the whole set and: the day begins with its first sunbeams, birds warble, roosters crow, dogs bark, human beings join in as they awaken to do their first daily tasks, adding little by little to the thousand and one sounds of the daily symphony, all tied together in the common rhythm of life.

When we take a close look at the course of existence around us, we see the infinity of rhythms that are united in perfect melodies and chords.

We can say that our daily labor has its own rhythm.

We normally sleep at night and perform our activities by day; of course, there are exceptions for labor tasks that must be performed during night hours, but this is not the majority of cases.

The human organism responds to its ancestral timetables with the many changes that occur inside the body during the day.

For instance, body temperature oscillates constantly and reaches its minimum in the morning and its maximum in the evening hours.

Bodily changes also occur with blood pressure, heartbeat, muscle strength, and even the ability to learn or work varies throughout the day.

We all are aware of its instability by our tiredness, the slowing of our inner rhythm, and lack of enthusiasm for many different things by the time sunset arrives.

The rhythm of life develops as a result of the evolutionary process, in accordance with the adaptation of living things to their environment.

Let's take the example of the solar light signal, which offers the succession of night and day, the seasonal changes, the fluctuation of the weather.

This occurs together with the interaction between animals and their respective habitats, all of which determines the vital rhythm of living things.

Hence, a certain group of animals adopted a regimen of

night activity, with sleep and rest occurring by day.

Others, who are generally the most developed, including human beings, rest by night and are active during the day.

In accordance with this day and night regimen, we develop our own rhythms for eating, sleeping, being awake, rest and work.

In actuality, there are over one hundred known physiological systems and three hundred biological processes and functions that have specific time phases, generally within the 24-hour day period.

All the signals of light, sound, temperature and other vital factors around us determine the rhythmic functioning of our organism.

It has been proven that if those signals are altered for 21 days, they will effect changes in our body rhythms.

An example of this alteration to our rhythm can be observed in a trip to Europe from the Caribbean, where the hourly time change causes a shift in our normal activity; we want to sleep when we should be awake, and vice versa.

I remember the last time I went to visit my father in Australia.

After a warm welcome, I collapsed in the bed that he lovingly had prepared for my stay.

Upon awakening, I was stunned to know that two days had passed since my arrival.

That certainly was a long and invigorating sleep!

My body needed to adjust to the vibratory frequency of that location.

And the hourly time change altered my personal rhythm.

The existence of modern man depends, to a large degree, on social factors in the rhythm of life: the economy, culture, transportation, even the city in which he lives and works, are often in contradiction with his biological rhythms which alter and cause constant stress in people.

When alterations to those rhythms are present, there is a loss of organic balance and the possibility of deteriorating health increases.

According to the observations of gerontologists - specialists in the human aging process- one of the factors that contribute to longevity, is the permanent stable condition of the organism's fundamental rhythms, such as:

- o an organized life with stable periods of work and rest;
- o an adequate diet at regular intervals;
- o restorative sleep.

To survive to old age in as healthy a condition as possible and still preserve the functioning of the body's natural defense system, it is necessary from an early age to lead a normal rhythmic life in order to establish and maintain a stable sleep pattern, alertness, diet, work and rest.

When we recover the rhythm of life, we can accomplish in two hours what before took four hours to do.

If we do this, what was difficult to understand before, will be understood at a glance because body and mind are clear, and energy is optimal.

We will feel healthy and radiant.

Every human being has *a rhythm that is appropriate to for him or her.* It is a special condition that is characteristic of that individual. *A movement.*

Or, as we commonly call it, *"the vibes"* that a person has.

Such is the power of this movement that causes us to see one person more beautiful than another; their "vibes" is what touches us first.

When we love someone, we love his or her rhythm, which essentially manifests itself through an intermediary: the heart.

We then love this person's heart through its rhythm.

When we love everyone, we love the rhythm in each one and we beat together in that movement.

It is with our inner beat that we create the melody of our life, that which makes us dance in the wheel of *constant changes.*

"Oye como va, mi ritmo...
Bueno pa' gozar, mulata.
Oye como va, mi ritmo..."

As Carlos Santana sings it, the lyrics of this song are based on these short words; however, we all know it for its great rhythm and good "vibes". ...*Shall we dance?*

3

Karma

"A great obstacle to happiness is expecting too much happiness."

—FONTENELLE

The Sanskrit word "Karma" signifies: cause and effect.

Today, it is used by many people to denote that every action has an effect or a posteriori cause.

Nothing is randomly disconnected in the universe.

Everything we have thought of, spoken or done becomes karma, and consequently produces a direct or indirect reaction in our lives.

The universal mind orchestrates all that occurs in thousands of galaxies with unalterable precision and intelligence.

Everything that happens to us is a result of everything that we have thought of at some point. To every action follows a reaction and to every cause follows an effect.

Nothing in the universe happens by chance.

All things that happen are intricately interwoven with intentions and events.

Our thoughts originate causes which will be followed by consequential effects.

Quantum physics proclaims that reality is created at every moment through the interrelationship between the creator and his broad spectrum of possibilities.

In accordance with the intensity of our thoughts, its connotative effect or impact will ensue into our lives.

Within the unified field, thoughts give form and shape to electrons, transforming their normal wave state into subatomic particles, to later precipitate themselves with weight and mass in the physical plane, as the final product of what was first thought.

Everything that the mind can conceive of, it can attain.

When a thought remains for a while at a certain frequency or intensity, it is transmitted to the universe.

Said thought generates a cause which magnetically attracts the similar.

Then, it is only a matter of time for the thought to materialize itself within the shape of the thought.

All human beings have been endowed with this tremendous power of creative manifestation.

Our desires are lifted in the form of thoughts or causes which generate an impact in the molecular universe, changing them into objects or effects.

Nature itself responds to our desires without much stress

or tension.

Solely by emitting our thoughts in close proximity to nature, we can see them manifested.

Some months ago, I experienced such a profound contact with nature that it utterly changed my perception of things and especially my view of everything that is around us.

Every day, I go out for a walk with my pets, Michael, a Golden Retriever who has faithfully accompanied me for the past eight years, and Rebeka, a mini Poodle, who is as passionate and loud as I am.

During our daily ritual, and while looking around along the path, I spotted a beautiful clover bush which had such a hypnotic effect on me, that from within my heart a profound inner wish emerged; a thought transmitted to the universe: *"I want a four-leaf clover!"*

I said this in a loud voice, and in that precise moment, I focused my eyes on the bush's interior to confirm that there, among thousands of three-leaved clovers, was indeed, a four-leaf clover!

My excitement and happiness was such that I continued to walk with profound joy in my soul and I even took a photo to send to my brother Dennis, who lives in Australia, and he can attest to my spectacular finding.

The following day, remembering the experience, I did likewise, and nature once again responded to my wish with another clover, and thus this astounding manifestation and connection with the earth continued to occur on every walk, uniting my desire with the tangible emotion of seeing how this was possible.

By merely asking the universe and divine mind, I received an almost immediate response that manifested itself in the physical and material plane, and that left me surprised and filled with joy.

I still preserve each of those clovers amongst the pages of my favorite books and I marvel in knowing that we can communicate in such special way with nature.

Whenever we desire to do so, we can interact with the environment and its natural elements.

Everything that surrounds us is connected with the cosmos and from that natural communion with the universe; our determined association with the elements is born.

This energetic and vibratory correspondence with the environment is identical for all the beings that inhabit the world and we will always be linked to some elemental correspondence object that will respond with a total sum of events in accordance with our evolutionary state and the energy plane in which we live.

Every day is the result of the previous day. One season follows the other.

Spring comes after winter, autumn after summer.

My left foot follows my right foot, and all events have an almost perfect cause and effect connotation.

Many times in our way of life, we move hurriedly to do our daily tasks and to fulfill needs as well as other people's, which leaves us little time to achieve this kind of connection with the environment.

Yet, by staying in touch with nature for only a few moments, we can give ourselves peace, harmony and energetic balance.

We can even replenish our energy and vitality.

At the beginning of autumn one year, we visited a medieval castle in Koblenz.

It is situated on a hilltop and to get there you have to traverse an entire forest.

We left the car in the parking lot and from there we started to climb through the breathtaking forest, filled with exotic plants, birds of all kinds and lofty trees that seemed to touch the clouds.

Upon arriving at the castle, we found ourselves surrounded by butterflies of all colors and sizes.

Melissa was so excited that she immediately suggested calling out to them.

So we turned our palms upward and began to summon them.

A few minutes later, one of them alighted on my hand and another one on hers.

Camilla impatiently ran after some, wanting to touch them, until it dawned on her that if she moved, the butterflies would also fly away.

And so she stood still, raised her hand and moments later, a gorgeous multi-colored butterfly landed on her palm.

Luckily, my video camera was turned on and I was able to shoot the spectacular event.

It was so magical to feel this connection with our microcosm.

After the incident at the castle, our house filled with butterflies as well, entering through the windows, and every night we took them outside lest they were trapped indoors.

The method and result was always the same: we summoned them to the palms of our hands and they came near.

It was perfect communication with nature's beings.

Through this connection to nature, our energy levels grow incrementally, increasing the atomic vibrations in our bodies, and thus resulting in a continuous transmission of high frequencies which intensify our perceptions, and our evolution, as well.

Hindus call Dharma, or *"the path of great truths,"* - the law that supports our learning, either in this life or in previous lives.

Buddhists use this very same word to mean *"protection"* - claiming that if one stays on the divine or correct path and if our deeds have been and are good, a positive effect of inner transformation and evolution will ensue into our lives.

Sometimes we believe that bad events occur under the

influence of this law of cause and effect.

We repeatedly hear: *"It is my karma."*

But we forget that although this law is in effect, the path of Dharma, or protection, will also reward us for all the good deeds that we do and will show us the virtue of the good that we do in our daily actions.

Everything depends on us and on our "choices".

Our *decisions* shape our destiny.

For example, if we look back to the past and observe some of the decisions that we have made in the last ten years and their consequential results, we become aware of the enormous power of such choices and their manifested effects in our present life.

Not only the impact that they have caused in our individual lives, but in some cases, within the society or as part of the whole, especially on those leaders who in one way or the other, have forged the destiny of a family, a company, a people.

In the journey of life, there are always goals that guide our steps.

Like a compass, these goals provide us with a sense of direction, indicating which way is our North or the best horizon to follow.

Having a personal compass would help us to better manage our "individual private times".

To find that compass and use it as a route guide, we could ask ourselves these questions:

- o   What are my goals?
- o   Where do I want to arrive?
- o   What does this decision mean to me?
- o   What should I be focused on?
- o   Which tools will I use on the road?

All of us have wishes and desires, but desire alone does not cause our destiny to be manifested.

It is emotion that drives us to "the goal" and what gives our desires *manifestation power*.

It is the impulse that takes us to heaven or to hell.

Our goals are primarily based upon our "needs" and essentially upon our "momentum" or perfect time.

Let's think about those needs.

To mention a few, they could be:

- o   Security;
- o   Significance;
- o   Connection or love;
- o   Growth or maturity;
- o   Contribution and commitment beyond ourselves or /transcendence

But then, if we are capable of tangibly materializing our thoughts and desires, why is it that we cannot accede to the happiness that we yearn for?

Could it be my karma?

How can we change it?

Or, as my friend Madeleine would say: When does it end?!

Can we transcend this karma here and now?

The word "éxito" -which means success in Spanish- stems from the Latin term "exitus" which signifies "exit" or "result".

It is also derived from "exire" which means "exit" or "salir" in Spanish.

Therefore, it belongs to the etymological family of the verb "go" or "ir" in Spanish, with the most positive meaning and connotation that we could ever imagine: prosperity, a beautiful and comfortable home, vacations, travel, financial security, a close-knit family, freedom from worries, fears or frustrations.

But above all things, success signifies "inner peace'- feeling good about ourselves and our daily actions.

Success means respect for one's self.

This is the respect that we are continually searching for, in the pursuit of happiness and in ways to satisfy our lives, all in perfect alignment with the hopes or life plan that we have.

Success means winning and achieving our goals in life.

And all human beings long for success, especially since most people dislike mediocrity and conformity.

There is a very practical Bible quote that teaches:

"Faith moves mountains." And also, *"Believe you can move them and you will".*

However, not many people believe they can do this, and consequently, no one does it.

This is a principle that we can apply to everything we intend to do.

The "belief" that we can attain a goal is the "drive" that generates the strength to achieve it.

It is not enough to just think about it.

One also needs to *believe it's possible*" and feel that attitude of "*I am and I can*" from the depths of your being.

Believing is the thermostat that regulates our life achievements.

People see and perceive in us what we perceive in ourselves.

The Talmud advises us: "We do not see things as they are, but as we are."

And Buddha adds: "*We are* what we think".

If we think that we are not worthy of success, then that very same energy will be perceived by others and will potentiate and impact our lives with the same predicament.

By regulating this positive attitude thermostat towards life, one can modify and redirect it.

If we vibrate in the creative energy of love and our thoughts are loving and altruistic, we will generate a reality that is akin to that powerful emotional and mental state.

When we vibrate in the frequency of love, *everything is possible!*

We have the capacity to activate and develop this wonderful energy of love through our way of living in the same manner that the elements of nature teach us.

Our physical body is a reflection of the splendor and perfection of our infinite universe.

It is a perfect entity composed of billions of cells that are focused on our health and well-being.

When we vibrate in love, we activate the innate love energy of every atom of our being, filling all the billions of cells with harmony, balance, wisdom, perfection, light and peace.

In this state of love, the level of vitality and purity in our bodies is extremely high.

The vibratory frequency of our energies is also very high, and thus we connect to our divine source, the perfect universe that contains us in synchronistic oneness and balance.

Our wishes and desires are commands decreed on these subtle planes of consciousness that become manifested with the same intensity of love with which we emitted them.

By activating this energy we integrate ourselves into the pure essence of our being.

In this manner, we consequently attract reciprocal energies which nourish us in return and help us in our achievements.

And as Tango Feroz says: *"Love is stronger!"*

4

Correspondence

To be, or not to be: that is the question: Whether 'tis nobler in the mind to suffer the slings and arrows of outrageous fortune, Or to take arms against a sea of troubles, And by opposing end them? To die: to sleep; No more; and by a sleep to say we end the heartache and the thousand natural shocks that flesh is heir to, 'tis a consummation devoutly to be wished. To die, to sleep; To sleep: perchance to dream: ay, there's the rub; For in that sleep of death what dreams May come When we have shuffled off this mortal coil, Must give us pause: there's the respect That makes calamity of so long life; For who would bear the whips and scorns of time, the oppressor's wrong, the proud man's contumely, the pangs of despised love, the law's delay, the insolence of office and the spurns that patient merit of the unworthy takes, when he himself might his quietus make with a bare bodkin? Who would fardels bear, to grunt and sweat under a weary life...But that the dread of

> *something after death, the undiscovered country*
> *from whose bourn No traveler returns, puzzles the*
> *will and makes us rather bear those ills we have*
> *than fly to others that we know not of? Thus con-*
> *science does make cowards of us all; and thus the*
> *native hue of resolution is sickled o'er with the pale*
> *cast of thought, and enterprises of great pith and*
> *moment with this regard their currents turn awry,*
> *and lose the name of action.*
> from HAMLET by WILLIAM SHAKESPEARE

The master Hermes Trismegistus asserts that "all information about a man can be found within a single drop of his blood," and that "within each man exists a representation of the entire universe".

With these words Hermes developed a deductive method that permits a glimpse into the grandeur of the created universe, where all levels of existence share the same essence, organized in a system of holograms within other holograms, until infinity.

It is evident that within a man there exist visible and invisible aspects.

We can all feel the physical body, but there is no way to see or touch a thought.

We can only assume its existence by the *effects* that it produces.

According to the Law of Correspondence, as it is in the microcosm here below, so it is in the macrocosm up above.

In outer space we can see physical objects, such as planets, solar systems and galaxies.

But it is not possible to discover through these objects, the mind that directs them.

Only by inference we can be certain that they exist.

Every cell of the macrocosm, whether it be named man, planet, solar system or galaxy, proportionately possesses the exact degree of intelligence it needs.

The interconnection between the cells and the mind that governs them is perfect; the whole affects the parts and the parts, in turn, affect the whole.

A man may be smaller than the most microscopic speck of dust in the galaxy, but if a human being changes, he invariably will be altering the very essence of the entire universe.

Everything around us in the material plane has been previously created by someone's mind.

Even our physical bodies are moulded and shaped by our very own thoughts. Our emotions are directed by our thoughts.

In like manner, our actions are products of our thoughts, whether they be conscious or unconscious, but they have been previously conjured up in our mind.

If we guide ourselves by this Law of Correspondence, we must verify *what it is* that we are attracting to our lives.

If we enjoy happiness and harmony, then we are generating positive thoughts that benefit us and have impact within the material world.

However, if our lives are lacking or troubled, we should be aware that perhaps our thoughts are duly the same.

All of us at birth possess an evolutionary program that is imprinted in our genetic code, our DNA.

This does not mean that our lives are irremediably pre-destined, since at a defining moment in our evolution we will be capable of creating a new reality, as long as this capability is determined by our "correspondence".

We are able to create a new reality if and when we first accept and live *according* to our correspondence, or if and when that course of action is the one that we should take in the here and now in accordance with our evolutionary program.

In this case, we have the capacity to "choose" our reality.

We may think that we would never choose negative things for ourselves, yet how many people around us do we know that spend all of their time cursing their lives?

I know a few.

It is those very same thoughts that attract negative situations and invite a series of disastrous events to their realities.

The more liberated our thinking is, the more we can develop our ability to intervene in and influence our reality.

It is important, therefore, to observe what it is that we are attracting to our lives.

In 1994, in Tokyo, Japan, Dr. Masaru Emoto began a research project that would reveal an important finding about the function of energy in our thought patterns.

Dr. Emoto took some photographs of water samples from a frozen fountain, which, when observed against a dark background under the lens of an electronic microscope, revealed a beautiful crystalline hexagon similar to a snowflake.

He also took other photos of polluted water samples and using the same process, he discovered that these particular photos depicted cloudy images that were devoid of any sharpness, and were completely inexpressive.

He later experimented with different water samples from different places and countries, and found that when sounds or positive intentions were applied to the water, the molecules were transformed by gathering light into their shapes.

The photographs displayed a broad range of luminous patterns that were similar to fabulous diamond crystals.

After taking more than ten thousand photographs of various water samples from different parts of the world and using different scope projections, Dr. Emoto asserts that "positive thoughts" are able to modify water patterns.

And, given that the human body is composed of 70% water, we could deduce that, if we were able to *communicate* internally with this water on a cellular level, applying positive thoughts to our entire being, we would have much more light and vitality.

Dr. Emoto also asserts that, in the light of these scientific revelations, human beings will soon be able to change their physical structure *in communion with their thoughts.*

As a result of his findings, many commercial companies have made use of this information developing water products denoting positive messages of vitality, energy and health.

Today, on supermarket shelves we see hundreds of brands of water products with flavors, colors and substances rich in nutrition and hydration, all promising to nurture and impart us with good health by consuming them regularly.

Even though water infused with positive thoughts may bring well-being and help us to feel better, it is not enough to fill our inner voids.

Rhonda Byrne produced a movie in 2006 that would have an impact on all kinds of audiences and would reflect a new revolutionary concept about the power of our thoughts and ideas.

The movie "The Secret" —based on the Law of Attraction— promoted the idea of creating a bridge of communication with the universal energy and mobilizing that quantum energy towards our thoughts in order to attain success in our lives.

According to the principles of "ask, believe and receive' the steps to achieve whatever you desire are:

1   Identify what it is that you want; then, ask the universe for it in the clearest possible way.

2   Focus your thoughts on the thing you desire and act as if you already have it in hand. Believe it is possible, and be grateful beforehand for its manifestation.

3   Be attentive to the synchronicities of life, as our requests can be manifested in many different ways. Therefore, we need to be open to receive its manifestations.

The movie included commentaries by well-known personalities from the medical, scientific, metaphysical and spiritual fields, who endorsed those same concepts and reinforced the idea that everyone can come to know the secret of happiness.

Apart from the impact created by this revelation, and the following it has from influential people, such as Oprah Winfrey, Ellen DeGeneres and Larry King, to name a few, who have already attained what they desired, were the very same promoters of this formula who have sold millions of products and sub-products, filled their pockets and made their dreams come true.

The rest of us mortals: *we just continue visualizing.*

5

Mind

> *"Begin by doing what is necessary, then, what is possible, and suddenly, you will be doing the impossible."*
>
> — St. Francis of Assisi

Do you believe that good or bad luck exists?

Having good luck is not an accidental element; it is not a supernatural realm outside of our control. Good luck is an individual power; we create it ourselves; it is first born in our thoughts, and later it is reflected in our actions.

There is no magic possessed by the so-called "lucky people", or those with supposedly "lucky stars".

On the contrary, what we see behind them are acts and realities, constant effort and desire to excel.

People who are said to be lucky are not lying in bed or locked up in their houses waiting for opportunities to appear...

no. They are always in motion, searching and finding, asking and receiving.

Good luck occurs in the presence of a "positive mind-set," state; a determination to focus on those specific, effective steps that we need to take in order to find the opportunities that will allow us to attain our goals.

If we classify someone as being lucky because she obtained the ideal job, we should keep in mind that this good luck is due to her thorough preparation for the job: having previously taken courses, searching for and applying for jobs, continuously submitting her resume, not being afraid of taking risks. Then, when the opportunity arose, she was ready and jumped at the chance.

Those who have found their ideal partner were not hiding in a hole waiting for their prince or princess to show up.

They dressed up, went out, conquered the fear of socializing with new people, joined a club, went to parties, and made friends. Then they prepared themselves emotionally, and when that special person came along they were ready for him or her.

Good luck does not come to us as a result of witchcraft, bindings or spells. Good luck comes when there is common sense, planning, determination, and intellectual preparation.

Good luck presents itself when we *mentally create it*, and when we come out, look for, and act upon it.

Germany, Winter 2009

One year during my childhood it seemed our luck had vanished altogether as we waited in vain for snow. Finally it began to snow! We had been waiting for the arrival of the white fluffy mantle that covered our mountains to show up.

It is so magical to feel the snowflakes brushing against my cheeks. When I was 11 years old, my family went to the Australian Alps.

For many years afterward, I could still remember how much I had enjoyed that trip and the excitement I shared with my sister, when we both rolled down the slopes and wallowed in the snow.

It was, perhaps, that particularly enduring *vivid thought* that magnetically brought forth this new image that I presently have before me.

I see Melissa and Camilla playing and sledding through the snow, expressing the same emotions and having the same fun that I used to have back then.

The snow has a strong and deep connection with the surrounding silence that cuts through us like a thunderbolt. It takes us through inner roads of profound introspection and self-analysis.

Covered up in my red scarf and sitting on the stairs that face the park, now covered with snow, I began to think about my life, about the lives of all human beings in general. I wondered if the striving and the long desired continual search for happiness is only making us feel more miserable every day?

Each day, we recite our positive affirmations and we drink our coffee in beautiful, multi-color mugs designed with inspirational messages like: *"Fly as high as your dreams"*.

We have bought a hundred volumes on how to become rich and successful with the Law of Attraction.

In fact, last year more than 5,000 titles were published about happiness and how to achieve it rapidly.

Most of the methods use the same formulas under different names; and so here we are, trying to incorporate these success models into our lives. But even after reading all the magic formulas on how to achieve great happiness, we feel increasingly impoverished and the emoticons with smiley faces that we use in our emails are only masks that hide our daily frustrations.

I remember a short tale by Jorge Bucay that said:

"There once was a king who visited his garden and discovered that his trees, bushes and flowers were dying. The Oak tree told him that he was dying because he was not able to be as tall as the Pine. When he went to see the Pine tree, the king found him disheartened because the Vine gave grapes and he could not. And the Vine was in sorrow, for she desperately wanted to blossom like the Rose. The Rose, in turn, wept because she was not as tall and sturdy as the Oak tree. He then came across a blooming and fresher-than-ever Daisy.

The King asked her: "How can you grow so healthy in this gloomy and sullen garden?" "I don't know. I must have always assumed that when you planted me, you wanted daisies. If you had wanted an Oak tree or a Rose, you would have planted them. And I then said to myself:, "I will try to be the best Daisy ever".

It is now your turn. You are here to contribute with your fragrant scent. Simply look at yourself. There is no possibility of you ever being another person. You can either rejoice in this idea and thrive, watered by the love for yourself, or wither away in your own despair and self-condemnation.

This happens to us many times.

We become withered by our own dissatisfactions and by our own absurd comparisons to others.

- *If only I were...*
- *If only I had...*
- *If only my life were...*
- *If only my family supported me...*

We are always envisioning an uncertain future, rather than enjoying the present time, stubbornly disregarding the fact that *happiness is a subjective and willful state of mind.* We can either choose to be happy with what we are and what we have, or we can live an embittered life for all that we do not have or cannot be.

We will only thrive by accepting that we are what we are; that God created each of us solely and uniquely, and that no one else will be able to do what we have come here to do.

Happiness is a choice that you can make whenever and wherever you want. Our thoughts, not our circumstances, allow us to feel our happiness.

You are the only person who is capable of controlling your thoughts and filling yourself with happiness. We need to learn to love what and who we are. Only when we *love* and *accept* ourselves as we really are, do we open our hearts to be loved by others. The most difficult path is the inner path. It is a path that we should travel on at least once in our lifetimes.

As I was travelling through France last year, I visited Chartres Cathedral. This edifice exhibits a majestic Gothic-style structure and the most significant aspect is that it was constructed over an original medieval Celtic building. It is still very well-preserved, and in its interior, a great and magical labyrinth can be found which leads us beyond that physical place, to spiritually connect us with what we were, are, and will be.

Chartres Cathedral very much resembles our inner labyrinth. When we enter into the labyrinth of our minds, we are able to quickly find our way out if we pay attention to where the entrance is, at the start of the journey. Once we are there, if we firmly *"believe"* we know where the exit lies, it will quickly reveal itself to us. If the fear of not finding our way out lurks behind, however, we might keep walking around in circles until someone shows up and prompts us to *"see"* where the exit is.

Once we are outside the labyrinth, we can say to our-selves: *"It was so easy! How could I not have realized it before?"*

Mental processes are similar to a labyrinth. Intelligence is inherent in life itself. This is an inborn quality in human be-ings, as it is in nature, but it is only that we have forgotten how intelligent we are. Our very social structure hampers our intelligence.

The intelligent person cannot be mechanically forced to do anything, as he will always question, reason, and choose. Therefore, a clever person may become a threat to the system because of his rebellious, assertive and individualistic nature.

Intelligent people have the capacity to resolve their own problems. The size of the conflict does not matter, as they can always rely on an infinite source of solutions.

Throughout human history, nevertheless, greedy and un-scrupulous human beings with a thirst for power, in the name of morality, have gradually instilled numerous fears in society to cause people to forget about their capacity to solve problems and about their precious uniqueness. We have be-come human clones, thus losing the connection with the in-nate intelligence imprinted upon our essence.

I once read an interesting anecdote that surely illustrates what intelligence is:

"One Catholic, one Protestant and one Jew were speaking with a friend who was diagnosed with a terminal illness, and only six months to live. "What would you do?" he asked the Catholic, "if your doctor gave you only six months to live?" "Ah," answered the Catholic, "I would donate all of my possessions to the church, take Communion every Sunday and pray the 'Our Father' prayer every day." "And what would you do?" the friend asked the Protestant. "I would sell everything, travel around the world and have a marvelous time." "And you?" he asked the Jew. "Me? I would go and talk with another doctor." Now, that's intelligence!

We enter this world free of contamination, and with pure intelligence. The pages of our life are blank and ready to be written upon.

Our society takes immediate charge of writing data onto our personal pages, thereby splitting up our own way of thinking and fragmenting our view of life. Whether one is Catholic, Christian or Communist, the society does not wait. The childlike innocence radiating from your being is immediately corrupted. Your wings are cut off and you are nor *dependent* on your parents in order to grow, lest it be possible for a child to be so intelligent and rebellious that he becomes self-sufficient and without need of his parents.

Parents enjoy their children's dependence on them. Their

lives become meaningful with this dependence. They now know that they are helping these children grow and that their lives are purposeful.

Parents feel creative and busy, and the more children they may bring into this world, the more children there will be to depend on the care they provide, and the happier the parents will feel with this dependence that fills all of their voids.

They are now so actively engaged in raising their children that they do not have the time to reflect on their own problems, and even though on the surface they may genuinely desire their children's independence, deep down they practically crave for this dependence from their children which serves to distract them from their own inner self-observations.

Independent children unintentionally hurt their parents with their sense of independence, as they do not seem to need so much of them.

These children are capable of solving conflicts on their own. They connect with the innate intelligence that has been molded in their programming since the beginning of human life. These children do not allow themselves to break because they "know" the way. Many parents feel frustrated when they discover that their children are so intelligent and independent, that they fear not being needed by them. For this reason, many parents subdue and destroy their children's intelligence, instilling fears and prejudices into their daily life of mediocrity.

Nobody likes rebels. Intelligence is rebelliousness.

Nobody likes to have their authority questioned and intelligence generally gives rise to doubts, questions, analysis and observations.

Everyone's living intelligence arises from doubts and questions. Why do some people live better lives than others? Why do some people with a high intelligence quotient, and who are successful in their given professions, are not able to apply their intelligence to their personal lives, floating adrift, going from suffering to failure, from glory to fear, completely out of balance? And why do others, who are also extremely intelligent, end up working for employers with a lower IQ, but who know how to connect, influence others and relate better?

I have met some people who might be classified as genius in regard to their intelligence, but are real failures in their private lives.

Many have not taken the risk of maintaining a loving relationship and have not married because they claim that most marriages finally end up in divorce.

Perhaps they have worked all their lives in utterly mediocre jobs, not wanting any more responsibilities or pressures and preferring to remain in a comfortable situation.

They have not cultivated positive friendships, since it is difficult for them to relate to intelligent people; and many have not taken the risk of investing in property or business -lest they should lose all of their money- and so on, and so forth. And the list goes on.

These people make use of all their brainpower to prove why things do not work, rather than using this power to *make them work...*

All of the negative thinking behind their actions contributes very little and creates nothing.

They exhibit enough brain capacity to be able to succeed in their lives, but they lack "thinking" power.

The key to this process lies in the emotions.

Normal human beings only use about ten percent of their total neural capacity.

Gifted people, like Albert Einstein, only use about twelve percent.

This offers us a vague notion of how enormous and unexplored our brain is and the capacities we could develop if it was used correctly.

Most probably, if we were to use more of this capacity, it would radically alter our perception of the world and of our own life.

Our senses, such as smell, taste, sight, hearing, touch, would become exacerbated and our perception and connection with the environment that we live in, would dramatically change.

It is of paramount importance to gain an understanding of what makes us happy or what we dislike what we are afraid of or delights us, what makes us move or paralyzes us.

How do these emotions exert influences on our thoughts, memories, perceptions or dreams? Are the emotions indelibly forged into our genes, unable to change their programming, or does the brain learn them from its environment?

We can observe that what we consider as the external brain, the cortex, is the location of the most sophisticated neural functioning.

Said functioning is essentially based on the growth of much more primitive structures that link us with our biological ancestors.

In the deepest area, specifically related to emotional aspects, is the insular lobe in the lateral temporal zone of the brain.

Emotions, feelings, memories, and everything that is associated with our affective functioning reside there, as well as anything that may trigger our reactions, impulses, and all that pertains to our instincts.

Prior to reaching the strictly human phase, where we think, reason and reflect, there are two areas which link us to the animal kingdom.

One is located in the posterior part of the brain, called the reptilian brain because it corresponds to the brain development in reptiles, where a part of our instinctual and impulsive structure resides and which causes us to react to any external stimulus, be it fighting or running away, trying to possess or escaping.

It allows us to adapt to and relate with the surrounding environment.

Additionally, there is the limbic zone of the brain, where a more subtle relationship begins to develop, causing us to feel the connection with the environment, and there emotions are born.

The left brain hemisphere controls everything that is sequential or that has to do with certain routines and essential logical elements. All that is normative learned or mechanical, whatever is standardized and classical, is situated in the left hemisphere of our brain.

The right hemisphere is the creative, dreamy, and artistically-oriented part of our brain.

Inadvertently, we have put aside the feminine aspect of our psyche, which creates relationships and lives through images, and has an intuitive and instantaneous vision, which is much more spontaneous and direct.

Over time, researchers have concluded that we need to work with both hemispheres because the common intersecting point between emotional intelligence and rational intelligence is the word "intelligence".

Throughout the twentieth century, a concept of intelligence prevailed that was virtually constrained to the intellectual functions, and a tool known as the "intellectual quotient test or IQ" was created. This test measures the cognitive functions of the brain, such as vocabulary, data knowledge, short-term memory, verbal reasoning, and ocular and manual movement.

Many people who have low scores on these tests are very successful in their lives, while others with a higher IQ have not succeeded as much.

What then, is intelligence? We could define it as the capacity to acquire new knowledge and apply it to new situations in order to resolve problems; the capacity to be innovative during processes of change, and the capacity to solve problems efficiently. It is also the art of understanding parameters and adapting to life. It does not consist of having the knowledge of many things. An encyclopedia knows about many different things, but even so, it is not intelligent. Computers have incredible memory, but this is not enough to be considered intelligent.

Intelligence must be tested against daily and tangible life situations, how we adapt to them, and how we move about in relation to the world that surrounds us.

Scientists have said that one animal is more intelligent than another when it knows how to better adapt to its ambient environment.

This principle of adaptation to the environment, as it relates to the human realm, makes a good connection with the principles of emotional intelligence.

In 1983, Howard Gardner, psychologist and Harvard University professor, influenced the world of education with his key work: "Frames of Mind – The Theory of Multiple Intelligences."

In actuality, it does not speak about intelligence, but about the intelligences. It is universally accepted today that a human being is capable of displaying a variety of different intellectual abilities from diverse sources of intelligence.

Two of the intelligence capacities as described and established by Gardner, the intrapersonal and the interpersonal constitute the foundation of a concept that other psychologists, John Mayer and Peter Salovey, named for the first time in a doctoral thesis, as "emotional intelligence".

According to Robert Cooper, emotional intelligence is the ability to handle one's own and other people's emotions, the capacity to feel, understand, control and modify one's and other people's moods. It is the capacity to control impulses, defer gratifications, and regulate our own moods without allowing our anguish to interfere with our rational thinking. It is the ability to relate, sympathize with and trust in other people.

Thanks to the work of Daniel Goleman, "Emotional Intelligence" - 1995, the concept of mind-frames is successfully introduced to the society; completely transforming the previous idea that intelligence only rests in the intellect.

This scientific research conceptually revolutionizes and sheds light on emotional functioning.

The word emotion is derived from the Latin word *emovere* that means: to be moved by. We are all constantly being moved, touched, and affected by everything around us at the same time, we are also affecting our surroundings.

By observing this behavior pattern in animals, we can say that the original function of the emotions, as illustrated by Charles Darwin in his work "The Origin of Species', is to prepare animals for action, especially in an emergency situation.

When in danger, all animals react abruptly. In seconds, birds fly away and mammals move rapidly to the fight or to flight.

These are basic impulses for the preservation of life. The majority of our emotions are recorded in our DNA.

In order to achieve emotional intelligence, the first thing we must realize is that there are no negative emotions.

Some emotions may be more agreeable than others, but all precisely inform us of the essence of the situation that we are experiencing at that moment. All emotions and feelings always have a reason for being. Not one is bad in and of itself; it just simply fulfills its function.

It has been found that among the principal biological changes that occur during a state of happiness, there is a boost of activity in the neural center, which inhibits negative feelings and favors an increase of available energy, and a diminishing of disturbing thoughts.

There are, however, no specific changes in the physiology, except for a sense of tranquility that makes the body recover faster from the biological awakenings of its baffling emotions. This setting offers the body a general rest, as well as a good and enthusiastic feeling to fulfill any task and to make an effort to attain many different goals.

According to several studies regarding the emotional intelligence in both men and women, men with high emotional intelligence are usually more socially balanced, extroverted, cheerful, and not prone to shyness or predisposed to worry.

They exhibit a gifted ability to commit themselves to causes and people, often take on responsibilities, maintain an ethical vision of life and have loving relationships.

Their emotional lives are rich and appropriate, they feel good about themselves, and are comfortable with their fellow human beings and the social universe in which they live.

In regard to emotionally intelligent women, they tend to be energetic, freely express their feelings, have a positive self-image; for them life always makes sense.

As it is with the men, these women are usually open and sociable, are able to adequately express their feelings without emotional outbursts that they would later regret, and can cope with high stress situations. Their social balance allows them to easily make new friends and they generally feel at ease with themselves enough to be cheerful, spontaneous and open to sensual experiences. They rarely feel anxious, guilty or overwhelmed by worry.

Now then, what differentiates people who possess emotional intelligence from those who do not?

The difference is that the majority of one's life desires, dreams or goals are linked to other people's participation in them.

No one is completely alone in life, and logically our plans for the future are always alternatively connected to the environment that surrounds us.

Therefore, if we are to achieve our goals or accomplish our objectives, we must develop and have this social capacity. This interaction is what allows us to advance toward our goals with much more confidence and trust.

Developing and implementing certain social capabilities is of vital importance due to the increasing complexities of contemporary life, in terms of having to deal with personal aspects; stress, conflicts, misunderstandings and disagreements. This occurs also in professional life, -in terms of having to contend with labor competition, customer service and devastating social and economic pressures.

These abilities allow us to efficiently lead other people, motivate ourselves and others to reach objectives, understand what is happening to us and in the environment around us, reconcile or mediate conflicts, influence other people within the sphere of our family or working life, and have a deeper understanding of our own and other people's needs.

Many religious groups justly motivate their members to achieve success in their lives via the confidence and support provided by those very same groups and many of them effect positive changes in their lives by utilizing this social energy.

Learning about our emotions helps us to develop our emotional coefficient. Today, communication with our surrounding environment is largely accomplished through technology and more specifically, the Internet. We communicate more easily by email or chat than personally.

But these means of virtual communication may also increase the probability of developing conflicts and misunderstandings.

We generally read positive and negative messages in a neutral way, perhaps without adding the emotional emphasis that the sender may want to express. The exchange of communication becomes exhausted in the written word. We cannot discern the tone, gestures, the facial look or energy of the other person and this produces fragility in the message.

The modality of receiving messages directly through our telephone causes us to respond right away without much reflection, which, in turn, may generate frequent misinterpretations.

Everyone interprets email messages via their own biases and expectations.

The writer overestimates his ability to be clear and thinks that his text only says what it means to say; however, we interpret his message according to what we unconsciously or consciously already had in mind and in accordance with the individual person's manner of expression.

We take for granted that the emotions expressed in our email message are obvious and easily understood by the reader because when we write it, we hear our own tone of voice and know what we intend to transmit. But what one person writes is not always what the other person reads into or interprets from what he reads.

Daniel Goleman argues that misinterpretation of email messages happens quite frequently because, apart from the emoticons that may be imbedded in the message, there really does not exist a channel to express what we truly feel. Even allowing for these differences in communication, may result in irreparable damage to once friendly relationships.

An email message may be dangerous in the hands of an impulsive person simply because when a situation turns out to be confusing, or when impatience grows for lack of an immediate answer, his feelings of insecurity can become elevated, thereby amassing internal tension, which can only be released by an outburst of anger directed at the message recipient.

But the relief does not last long. When he calms down and evaluates the situation with a more tolerant outlook on what has happened, it is already too late. The message has been converted into a two-directional weapon: it hurts the recipient, as well as the sender.

The mismatch between what was meant to be said and what the other understood also has to do with the fact that the transmitter and receiver of the message do not share the same context: they each read and write in a different time and space, under the inescapable influence of their current state of mind and the background of their relationship up until that moment.

Email is not an adequate means to deal with delicate matters. It should not be used to clarify an annoying or conflict situation.

On the other hand, we also can create false expectations by reading messages or emoticons on those days when we are more inclined to romance.

In fact, there are well-known stories of people who developed an instant crush on someone after having read an email message and then projecting their own desires and needs on that which moves or inspires them.

It has happened to me! I read an email and, all of a sudden, I find myself falling in love with the author without even knowing who he really is and on what part of the planet he lives.

It is possible to feel *personal synchronicities* over what you have read and from there, create an enchanted fairy tale situation and fantasize about a physical encounter with that person. Days later, you admit that although so-and-so writes like the Greek gods of Mount Olympus, your lives are separated by diverse geographical, cultural and social oceans, and that, in reality, you share very little in common so as to tear down those barriers, except for the cybernetic compatibility enclosed in an email message.

Some people are lucky enough to read emails from other people that at least live in their neighborhood.

Such is the case of my friend, Sonia, who fell hopelessly in love with Bob.

Bewitched by the subliminal charm of his beautiful words, she invented various characters with secret email addresses in order to get to his heart, and in this incessant effort, she discovered her enormous capacity to love and the courage to generate changes to make her life meaningful.

Beyond the love that she conquered, she managed to conquer herself and tear down old paradigms that constrained her interaction with the environment around her.

In this case, the email was the catalyst for a real and positive internal change. Although, of course, as in any love story, there were floods of tears and sad emoticons.

Many times when we write, and depending on our mood that day, we find it easier to say things that we otherwise might not dare to say face to face.

This can cause a lot of confusion and frustration for the person who writes, as well as for the person who reads.

In this means of communication, the facial looks and body language which tangibly accompany an emotion are not present. Neither is the tone of voice that can make a word sound positive or negative, and, perhaps the most important, the touch which makes us speak in silence and understand the other beyond a thousand spoken words.

There are also cultural gaps and idiomatic expressions that may be misinterpreted through internet communication or simply may not impact the other person with the same intensity as it was written.

However, in these last few years of our technological revolution, we have learned a good deal about different world cultures and we have torn down many paradigms in our human society. Statistically speaking, the quality of three out of every ten marriages have been affected by the Internet and fifteen percent of those married couples have had to move to other cities in order to live together with their partner.

We have left our tribes to conquer new spaces and relate with very diverse cultures. Our task is to join forces and walk side by side towards our goals.

Whenever two or more people join together in a spirit of collaboration and respect, the synergy that is based on communication and empathy will manifest itself naturally.

But then, where is *happiness?* Will it be in another country? With people that perhaps speak other languages?

We wonder about this many times, because as with the daisy in our earlier tale, we believe, that if we were in another place, our life would be better.

Jesus once said, "Not a leaf falls from the tree unless the Father, through His laws, decrees it".

Thanks to this truth, we understand that we are not a leaf that is subject to the capricious winds of chance.

We forge our own future according to the thoughts we have.

The entire universe is a conjunction of thoughts that emanate from the infinite mind of God.

We share in His infinite mind and from it we originate ideas that we later can apply to the world of shapes and forms.

6

Generation

> *"What if you slept,*
> *And what if,*
> *in your sleep you dreamed?*
> *And what if, in your dream,*
> *You went to heaven*
> *And there plucked*
> *A strange beautiful flower?*
> *And what if, when you awoke,*
> *You had the flower in your hand?*
> *What then?"*
>
> — DEEPAK CHOPRA

Feminine and masculine principles are ever present in all of the universe's phenomena.

The subconscious, or subjective mind, corresponds to the feminine aspect, whereas the conscious, or objective mind, is attributable to the masculine aspect.

In the material plane, we tend to see generational issues in the form of gender.

In accordance with the masculine or feminine genre, carnal manifestation of life is generated.

Within the animal and plant kingdoms, this life-generating principle is continuously observed.

The entire universe respects their feminine and masculine genders.

Beyond their respective sexual characteristics, human beings are carriers of feminine and masculine energies.

We should strive to effect the best harmonization of these forces in order to attain the balance which will bring joy into our lives.

The union of both feminine and masculine energies is necessary in order to create something new. It is in the development of these two polarities where one finds the perfect balance for the manifestation of creativity.

In the Far East these two energies are called the Yin and the Yang, and in the Toltec culture they are referred to as Tonal and Nagual.

In his work, "Tales of Power", Carlos Castaneda describes the explanation of these concepts rendered by his teacher, the sorcerer Juan Matus.

Matus related that the *Totality of One's Self* consisted of two components of the individual being: the Tonal and the Nagual. *"Every human being has two facets, two different entities,* two 'counterparts' that become operative at the moment of birth; one is called 'Tonal' and the other 'Nagual'.

Matus maintained that the Tonal was the organizer of the everyday world, the one who took charge of bringing order to the chaos of this material world.

All that we know and do as human beings is the work of the Tonal. All that we can name, verbalize or define is part of the Tonal.

The Tonal is all that we can ascertain through our senses. It is all that our eyes can perceive. It begins at the moment of birth and ends at the moment of death. We could say figuratively that the Tonal *"constructs the world"*. Its function is to judge, evaluate, and witness.

Although truthfully, what the Tonal does is to formulate the rules that allow us to capture and comprehend the world in such a way that it becomes *"coherent and logical"*.

There exists a Tonal individuality for each of us, and then there is a *"collective"* one for all of us at any given time, which is called the *Tonal of the times*.

Castaneda illustrates this by defining the Tonal as an island where we accumulate a number of unnecessary objects which draw our attention.

The island is considered the only thing that exists, and any indication coming from *outside* of the island, or as the Toltecs called it: from the Nagual, is discarded by the Tonal, which insists on denying the *exterior* existence, using at its disposal a powerful tool known as: *reasoning*.

Anything that is considered *not reasonable* and which cannot resist the scrutiny of the intellect is rejected as impossible, and consequently its existence as *real* is denied.

The cleaning out of the island, or Tonal, of all unnecessary things such as dense emotions (hatred, jealousy, anger, etc.), harmful habits (use of tobacco, alcohol or drugs) and other bad practices, is the first task that an apprentice of these sciences must tackle, and thereby acquire a tremendous store of energy that will allow him to visualize *beyond the island* and capture the subtle signals that emanate from the exterior, or Nagual.

The Nagual is the part of us that we never deal with, since we are more accustomed to *like* the sweet and bitter fruits of the everyday world. We obsess over them, rather than connect with that impassive wisdom, watching the game of life like the spectator of a movie who learns from its projection without getting involved as an actor or character.

The Nagual is that part of us for which there is no description, words, names, or knowledge.

It is the "magical" part of us which we access rarely. Contrary to our intellect and reason, its essence resides in the scope of creativity, of fantasy and intuition, gifts considered useless by the Tonal, but highly appreciated by artists who use them to create majestic works that will endure for all time.

At birth, and for some time afterwards, we are all Nagual.

During this time, we feel the need for some sort of counterpart to what we have in order to function. We lack the Tonal and from the very beginning, it imparts a feeling of not being complete.

At this point, the Tonal begins to emerge and eventually develops to a magnitude of such absolute importance to our functioning that it overshadows the Nagual's radiance, subjugating it, and thus we become all Tonal.

From the moment one becomes all Tonal, we do nothing but increase that old sense of incompleteness; the same sensation that accompanies us from the moment of birth and constantly tells us that there is another part of us that would make us whole.

From the moment we become all Tonal, we begin to make pairs. We feel our two sides, but we represent them with objects from the Tonal. We say that our two parts are the soul and the body. Or mind and matter.

Or good and evil. God and Satan, flowing rhythmically with the life generation of the Almighty.

***

"Mirror, mirror, on the wall, who is the prettiest of them all?"

In the popular story, "The Fisherman and His Soul", Oscar Wilde described "the mirror of wisdom" in which all the things of heaven and earth were reflected, except for the face of the one who looked at himself in it. It would not reflect him so that whoever was to look at himself in the mirror would become wise. All the other mirrors were merely mirrors of *opinion*.

Those who possessed the mirror of wisdom knew everything.

One of the most important texts of alchemy is called Sefer Mar'ot or "the book of mirrors". It is a work which highlights the use of mirrors as a tool to transform the philosophical stone.

The mirror is the object that permits us to see ourselves and to see how others see us.

In the ancient past, mirrors were used in magic rituals and initiations for their connection with other dimensions. They are believed to be "doors" that open to the soul and many traditions tell about legends of spirits who have been trapped in the light of a mirror. Also, it is said that vampires cannot look at themselves in a mirror because their mere reflection would annihilate them.

However, a mirror has a surprising power of showing us who we are. By looking at ourselves in the mirror, it may help us in that encounter with our true essence.

In the Temple of Apollo at Delphi, the priests engraved a revealing inscription that reads *"know thyself"*.

Carl Jung remarked in his book, "Meeting the Shadow" that *"meeting oneself could be a very unpleasant experience"*. But even so, happiness is derived from this *meeting with our polarities.*

The acceptance of these two forces, working in communion and balance, will help us to make possible our ideal.

Finding our shadow will cause our light to be more powerful in order to see our way, and thus, not be lost.

The Wheel

> *"Of all the wheels, there is only one that now and then, ignored by its subtleness inclines the balance, the straight beam; the luck that is, capricious as the moon.*
> *See her sleep in her silvery cradle, subject to thousand eternal variations, plenty of hanging milky light, whether for or against the fortune."*
> —JOSÉ BENITO MARTÍNEZ

Living life in *plenitude* is a very high and legitimate aspiration that is worthy of being achieved. Whoever loves life aspires to abundance and transcendence.

As human beings, we always search for transcendence as an ultimate end; to engender some good deed that will endure throughout time. This could be a seed planted in the earth, a footprint implanted and embodied in our society, in our family, in history.

People who love, respect and cause their lives to grow in all directions, are creating a positive synergy in the cosmic wheel of their existence.

What we do with our own lives is a decision that each one of us makes, but even so, life will continue to be the best of all gifts.

Life is our most valued possession since it has been given to us in liberty and freedom.

To avoid an unbalanced development of our life, we need to acknowledge its fundamental characteristics: life is plural, diverse, multidimensional, broad, varied, open and unlimited.

By keeping these features in mind, we can be aware and cognizant of the great measure that a human being is able to impart for himself and others.

Our life resembles a wheel. The wheel is always turning. Each time a change occurs, whether it is voluntary or not, whenever chaos ensues or there is a crisis, a loss, a separation, we are filled with worry, anxiety, fear and insecurity.

We eventually overcome the circumstances and hope again arrives to renew us with energy, optimism and joy.

My grandmother Ana used to lovingly cheer me up by saying *"the sun rises every day"*.

If we are suddenly enshrouded in overwhelming darkness, we must know and remember that at the turning of the wheel, the light will return once again.

It will always come again!

As the wheel rotates, bringing changes at every step, we cannot remain in *permanent states of happiness,* but we can indeed control how we respond to the change experiences.

Change appears without anticipation or planning.

As a case in point, it will always represent a learning experience which further makes possible our evolution.

In our wheel of life, a spiritual force exists that steers us towards hope and success. Faith is the motor that drives the wheel.

In essence, life is an invitation to balanced growth and healthy, harmonious and comprehensive development.

Defining a global vision of what we want to do with our lives is a stimulating and very useful prerequisite to charting our course.

We can choose a life with speedy, but limited successes, or we can aspire to a life that will harmonize short-term and long-term achievements in all aspects of existence. This challenge invites us to take action in various dimensions.

The physical dimension, the bodily base of existence, includes the necessary care to maintain our body in good condition to enjoy health and physical well-being.

This dimension requires us to consider a healthy diet, adequate rest, good personal hygiene, stress management and systematic physical exercise, which provides resistance, strength and flexibility.

Investing time and energy in the betterment of this dimension is highly prudent as it impacts our ability and capacity to work, adapt and enjoy life.

By renewing our physical dimension, we acquire sufficient energy and vigor to undertake whatever we propose to do.

Moreover, people who take care of their physical dimension positively modify their self-concept and thus increase their self-esteem and self-confidence. They feel much more predisposed to take advantage of the opportunities that cross their path.

The mental dimension includes the constant exercise of our mental faculties and its application to different life circumstances.

This dimension puts us in contact with the ideas of great thinkers and allows us to enjoy them, as well as develop our own intellectual forms of expression. Here resides the intellectual richness and quality of our thoughts which tend towards excellence.

The development of our mental dimension means to exercise, train, polish and broaden our mind in order to face life's challenges.

The spiritual dimension is the nucleus of our life because this is where our deepest and most cherished principles and values are situated. It is one of the richest dimensions, as it provides us with permanent evolutionary well-being.

This dimension is also the center of our own personal leadership because, within it, the path and direction of our entire life is defined. In this dimension, the meanings that permeate our existence with significance, value and purpose are originated.

Some of the ways and means that allow us to perfect our spiritual dimension are meditation, deep prayer, literature, music, art and communion with nature- the connection with the symbols that are around us.

When we embark on spiritual renewal, we penetrate into the leadership center of our life and we identify more with our beliefs and values;, and we renew our commitments.

The human being is, by nature, a social entity. We could say that it is a duty and a necessity to enter into contact with others in order to attain a large measure of emotional richness.

Everything, from the way we talk, dress, behave, and interact, is important in our contact with other people. Through this personal contact, others can influence us and we can influence them.

As individuals, we are endowed with a special gift.... the ability to "feel".

Feeling is what gives flavor to life; it serves to remind us about the joyfulness of being human, special and privileged. Thanks to our feelings, we maintain the bonds that tie us to others.

The social-emotional dimension is only developed when it is utilized, implemented and renewed through the interpersonal relationships which are initiated within our closest circles: family, friends, and society. These groups reach out to the farthest circles: country, the continent, the world. We are all part of a system, since as individuals we are able to influence other people.

As such, we should seek to act with integrity and collaboratively work as a team in pursuit of the same objective. Together we help, contribute serve, support and grow with others.

The family dimension is initiated through the encounter of two individuals who love one another. They respect and support each other through thick and thin, and create a permanent bond which carries them into the future with meaningful purpose.

This relationship leads to mutual development by nurturing confidence, commitment and acceptance. From the love that grows, the union may bear fruit in the form of children.

That is how a family is originated; a system of individual people that share sentimental, social, physical and spiritual bonds.

A functional family is cultivated and strengthened by the exercise of good communication, acceptance, good disposition, and acknowledgement of every member's efforts. They share dreams and realities, and support each other's personal and family development. All members of a family can learn from the other members.

The experience of living in a family becomes more formative if each member's unique and positive characteristics are recognized and developed.

Then, the dimensions of our human nature comprise a single unit. They are not isolated elements but constitute a synergistic unity.

The family members are like the two sides of the same coin.

The actions carry out in each dimension will impact the others in the group.

If our work is positive, our lives will be fruitful.

Conversely, if we are neglectful of any dimension and of the roles we play therein, our lives will be negatively affected, and we will not be able to reach the success that we are called upon to achieve.

The reality is that a real and deep interdependence of the dimensions exists.

The balance in our five dimensions guarantees a holistic and integrated human development, borne out of personal excellence and lasting success.

The Wheel affords us the possibility to grow continuously and yet never arrive, to only transcend in the experience of being and enjoy each phase with its consequential impact and teachings.

Cycle after cycle, it rhythmically rotates with our heartbeat in perfect balance and union with the environment.

Happiness does not consist of *arriving*, but of walking, being and *feeling* the communion with totality and wholeness.

It is in this walk that we feel our fullness, at peace with our essence, accepting and embracing every test as an evolutionary challenge that permits us to grow and awaken, and become more aware of just how precious our existence truly is.

It reminds me of the poem, "At Peace" by the Mexican poet, Amado Nervo:

"*So close to my sunset, I bless you, Life for never giving me deceptive hope, unfair work or undeserved sorrow since I see at the end of my harsh path I was the architect of my own fate; if I extracted honey or gall out of things it was for the sweetness or bitterness I added when I planted rosebushes I always harvested roses... Certainly, after my fresh youth the winter will come But you never told me May was eternal! No doubt I found long nights of grief But you did not promise me only good nights though I had some saintly peaceful ones I loved, I was loved, the sun caressed my face Life, you owe me nothing! Life, we are at peace!*

Polarity

I ""*Everything in creation is twofold. Everything has its opposite.*"

P olarity is the mechanism through which the universe maintains its state of balance.

By observing the flow of everything that surrounds us we can better understand it.

At a subconscious level, our body *knows* that our involuntary reactions always unify its polarity to obtain better results.

If we run forward, our body first moves backward. If we spring upward, our body is inclined to first go downward. If by crying we let all our tears come out, we will start laughing, and if by laughing we reach extreme laughter, then we will cry.

Like a pendulum, we constantly oscillate from one extreme to the other because we do not understand that if we totally polarize ourselves to one side, life will automatically swing us back to the opposite extreme. This occurs because our task is to learn by way of contrasts.

For example,: we know what light is only because we have seen total darkness before. Sadness gives relevance to joy. We can understand what goodness is, if the concept of evil exists. Disease gives us a clear perception of what health is.

For that reason, every situation that a human being lives through is of equal value.

The fact that our experiences are either pleasant or unpleasant is not important; what really counts is the wealth of wisdom that every experience provides to us.

Once we accept that, we will voluntarily proceed down the middle path because we will apply the good cook's seasoning to every aspect of life: add a pinch of sugar to the salty dishes and a pinch of salt to the sweet dishes.

We will then acknowledge that there may be some ugliness in beauty and some beauty in ugliness, some truth in a lie and some lies in a truth.

Opposites are the two extremes of the same thing. A mental state can be changed by focusing its attention on the opposite state.

The Almighty and the multitudes are the same; the difference resides only in the degree of mental manifestation.

If we observe the physical plane, we find that heat and cold are of identical nature; the difference is a matter of degrees.

The thermometer displays the degrees of temperature in which the inferior extreme is called cold and the superior one, heat. Between them are many degrees of heat and cold. There is no absolute reading on the thermometer that indicates where heat ceases and cold begins. All is reduced to more or less high or low vibrations. They are two poles of the same thing. The terms are relative.

The same happens with directions. If we travel around the world towards the east, we will arrive at a point that is west. If we travel north, we will soon find ourselves travelling south and vice versa.

Light and darkness are opposite poles of the same thing with many degrees between them.

The musical scale is the same. Starting from SI onwards we will come to find another SI, which continues infinitely. The differences between the extremes are nothing but a matter of degrees.

The same happens on the color scale, the vibratory intensity being the only difference that exists between red and purple.

Big and small are relative concepts. It is equally so with noise and silence, hard and soft. Positive and negative are the two poles of the very same thing, with numerous gradations between them.

What is *good* and what is *evil?*

They are not two absolute things, only that one extreme

we call good and the other evil, depending on the meaning that we want to give them.

Love and hate are considered diametrically opposed, completely different. But in keeping with the principle of duality, we can see that there is no absolute love or absolute hate different from one another. Both are nothing more than terms applied to the two poles of the same thing.

When we understand that mental induction is possible, that is to say, that mental states can be produced via other people's induction, then we recognize how we can communicate to another person a certain kind of vibration or polarity, thus changing the polarization of the entire mind.

The majority of results achieved through mental treatments are realized according to this principle.

For example, if a person feels sad, melancholic and fearful, a psychotherapist could elevate his own mental vibration to a desired level by means of his previously trained will, and thereby attain the required polarization in his own mentality.

Hence, via induction, he can produce an analogous mental state in the patient, intensifying the latter's vibrations and the person becomes polarized to the positive pole of the scale rather than to the negative one. Hence, his fears, melancholy and sadness are alchemically transformed into positive values such as contentment, satisfaction and similar inner moods.

Some meditation on this matter will lead us to the conclusion that almost all of these mental changes are affected along the lines of polarization, which is more of a question of degree than of kind.

The functional knowledge of polarity will better help us to understand our own mental states, as well as that of others.

By understanding that the difference in those states is purely a question of degree, and also by confirming this very same fact, we are able to elevate our inner vibrations at will, beneficially changing our polarity and its vibratory frequency, thus mastering our thoughts and consequent reactions.

Moreover, this knowledge permits us to intelligently help others by changing their polarity through appropriate methods.

The correct understanding of the principle of polarity can shed much light in order to solve our problems.

In his book "Man's Search for Meaning", Victor Frankl asserts that paradoxical intention works successfully in psychotherapies to combat anxiety caused by obsessions and phobias, specifically, the one known as anticipatory anxiety which precedes any challenge, such as public speaking, proposing marriage, avoiding sexual dysfunctions, or falling asleep.

Many times we can just think, *"What is the worst thing that could happen to me in this situation?"*, and then mentally and emotionally place ourselves in that supposed position or even wish that it would happen. It requires a little sense of humor, but it works.

This technique is based on the fundamental premise which asserts that, desire and fear are mutually exclusive, so if you desire what you fear, you can overcome the situation.

Think of the famous Murphy's Law which says: "If any-thing can go wrong, it *will* go wrong."

We could adopt a "positive" attitude by thinking of the misfortunes that might happen to us. We would be automat-ically reversing the opposites to that projection.

A frequently quoted example of this tendency to emphas-ize the negative is that every time a slice of bread spread with butter falls to the floor, people tend to vividly remember the times it fell with the buttered side to the floor, because if it were to fall with the buttered side up it would have fewer consequences.

Therefore, one gets the impression that bread always falls with the buttered side down, without considering the real probability of each occurrence.

Laws like Murphy's are the direct expression of such per-versities in the order of the universe. There is a mathematical study that confirms that, indeed, there is a greater probabil-ity that the toast will fall on the buttered side, but it is due to other factors.

I am now left thinking about another one of Murphy's Laws that says: *"The probability that you will stain your clothes while eating is directly proportional to the need that they remain clean."*

9

The Ideal

> *"Those who know how to look at life with optimism and stay on the path, can experience happiness and offer it to others".*
>
> —DALAI LAMA

The Dalai Lama tells us that mood is very important in order to be happy, and that true happiness cannot be confused with pleasure; rather, it is associated with the mental state that is achieved whenever a person liberates himself and no longer experiences suffering.

We can be happy when we obtain what we want, but soon we become accustomed to the new situation and slip back to our previous state of affairs,; all because human beings have the capacity to adapt themselves to new situations and then revert back to their habitual state.

The same thing happens when tragedy strikes us; at first we are gloomy and sad, but ultimately we return to feeling the same as before.

The intent to think in positive terms can have an immediate effect on our mood. More so, it consists of proposing well-being and happiness to one's self from the time we get up in the morning, in order to notice a drastic change in our lives.

The Dalai Lama asserts that an inner source of happiness is *self-esteem*. Personal dignity based on material things may end one day and it is necessary that one's own self-esteem becomes rooted in other personal attributes such as empathy, warmth and the ability to give affection.

You can only give that which you already *possess*. For he who does not have love is unable to give it and cannot receive it, if he does not project it.

As I mentioned before, we attract what we are or have.

According to the definition from the Royal Spanish Academy, "ideal" from the Latin word idealis, means: *"pertaining or relating to an idea, existing only in thought, fitting perfectly into a form or archetype;. excellent, perfect in its lines, perfect model that serves as a standard in any domain."*

The word denotes a subjective model which reflects our idea of what we seek and want.

Depending on that model, each person's ideal will be different in accordance with his *individual and unique* self-projection.

What then is our *Ideal* of happiness?

Therefore, happiness, is that which bears a resemblance

to what we desire from the deepest reaches of our thoughts and which is different for everyone.

It is that with which we *dream* and *invent* our present-day and future reality.

The reality we live is the one we imagine.

After all, the idea of what we are and seek is what gives *meaning* to our life and manifests itself in the reality of our existence.

We are what we project ourselves to be and we live as we imagine.

It is, therefore, important to live our possible ideal at every moment.

We do this by building our happiness upon the basis of what we *want and can attain.*

The ideal is the projection of our soul's essence which strives to live out its terrestrial experience in this dimension.

The driving force of our vital thinking is what leads us to find what we are searching for in the world of possibilities.

When we do not project this *ideal of being,* we feel lost in the ocean of life; we lack the ambition to *accomplish our goals.*

People who have achieved large success in their lives remark that what mobilized them towards their objective was their *"dream".*

When we dream of what we desire, we are manifesting it, creating it from our thoughts, giving it shape to an ideal of life or being, and molding it from the conscious level which knows that "making it happen" is totally *possible*.

Without dreams, our life becomes boring and monotonous, without any kind of challenge to discover.

While awake we can dream of the world that we seek, or we can dream in our sleep and from that reverie visualize possible universes.

In the past, dreams were believed to be the conduits by which the gods communicated with mortals, predicting future events, conceiving unusual universes, infernal or angelic visions, mysterious personages or marvelous events.

Within the Jewish culture there is a traditional ceremony called *"Hatavat Halom"*, which literally signifies: *making the dream good.*

Through this ritual, disturbing dreams can be transformed into positive interpretations that the rabbi is able to decipher in favor of the dreamer.

When we dream the mind's door is opened, thus allowing our desires, hopes, and ambitions to emerge, transporting us to "realities" beyond the scope of logic but which have a substantial impact on our experiences.

Dreams connect the physical body, the mind and the spirit.

Sigmund Freud, the originator of psychoanalysis, stated that, *"The emotions that are buried in the unconscious rise up to the conscious level during dreams. The world of dreams is a place which the spirit and the soul visit every night."*

He also asserted that, "Sleep is not merely somatic activity; it is a realized psychic phenomenon to fulfill desires and, therefore, it should be included in the grouping of comprehensible action —not incomprehensible ones— of our waking life, constituting the result of a highly complicated intellectual activity."

During sleep, the ethereal body separates from the physical body, which is necessary so that the vital body can repair the physical body.

In the Bible we can find close to seven hundred references about dreams as God's chosen way to transmit His Word.

Asleep or awake, we dream continuously.

From the dream we come and towards the dream we return.

Every awakening represents a renewal of the human project from the very instant that the conscious mind returns to reality.

In order to determine what our ideal is, we should connect with our childhood experiences, since that is where the archetypes of our ideal being begin to be implanted.

It may be useful to keep a diary with annotations of events that occur in our daily life that markedly show a pattern of conduct which will later help us to revise our image of the ideal imprinted in our essence.

We can constantly test ourselves with those things that bother us or that we dislike, and that too will give us a guideline regarding what we do not want as an ideal.

In this manner we bring to our higher consciousness the inner fire which does not permit us to fall into the deep sleep where we can *"live our dream"*.

The fire is always uncomfortable for some type of situation. It is full of questions about who we are and, why we are here. It challenges us with its questions at every moment and does not let us sleep so that we may *dream*.

By observing that which bothers us we can comprehend the nature of this inner fire so as to harmonize it with our ideal.

When we take note of the blueprints that happen in our life, we can systematically know more about what lies within our ideal archetype.

The more light we bring to that observation the more rapidly the inner fire will burn.

The intensity we bring to that work is quite important, as it gives us the key to open the door of higher consciousness towards what we are seeking.

Toltec wisdom states that when we access the deep reverie of our higher consciousness we receive "super powers" - we are aware of this abstraction because there, we can fly, go through walls, change our gender, and transform ourselves in the manner that we desire. In this *reverie* we are telepathic, *as we also are* in the reality that we live.

We have all read and learned that by vibrating in energy

of higher consciousness, we also activate these higher mental faculties.

Similarly, it is these super powers that cause us to again fall into an ordinary dream, robbing us of the possibility for *reverie.*

Because when we use these super powers for personal *pleasure,* we are "forgetting" about the consciousness of "being" - and so we once again fall into the ordinary dream's frequency.

We sever the *supreme power of manifestation.*

The same thing happens in real life when we go about experiencing and learning about ourselves.

We eventually come to a point where we have acquired an almost total comprehension of who we are and what we want; everything begins to open in our lives and, we have access to what we are searching for. But it is at that precise moment when we again *fall* into an ordinary dream, losing the possibility of utilizing that higher consciousness for that awakening in our evolution.

It was through this intricate and delicate internal process that the Toltec people understood the manner by which to access other dimensions and they did not allow themselves to be trapped by this evolutionary game where the ego can cause us to fall at a moment when we least expect it.

The trick is to stay *awake* during the reverie in order to explore other alternative realities.

The intent is to *guide the will* or intentionally guide the energy of the alignment of consciousness.

The will is a blind, impersonal and uninterrupted explosion of energy that causes us to behave as we do. The will is responsible for our perception of the everyday world.

Consciousness of being is mastered by breaking down the barriers of one's own perceptions.

In order to do so, we need to *align* the consciousness.

Upon reaching a certain depth, a barrier is shattered and the ability to align the emanations of our soul is momentarily interrupted. That situation is experienced as a perceptual void. The alignment is the force that has to do with everything.

By turning off the internal dialogue and eliminating the mental inventory we are able to "see" the human essence and project it from the will of the *conscious dream*.

Tibetan Buddhists over a thousand years ago, for example, perfected a method to dream while in a conscious state that even today is still a core part of this tradition.

Moreover, Aristotle in his work about dreams remarked that *"on some occasions, while we are sleeping, something arises in our consciousness suggesting that what we are seeing before us is a dream"*.

In the year 415 AD, Saint Augustine described two lucid dreams of a Roman doctor by the name of Genadio. This is the earliest recorded description of a lucid dream of which we have knowledge about. The term lucid dream is used in reference to the ability of becoming aware that one is having a dream.

So, how can we manage to have those lucid or conscious dreams?

We might say that, regardless of the method employed, the key is to develop those qualities necessary to remember dreams until we are able to remember at least one dream per night. Then, if we have a lucid dream we will recall it.

We may also familiarize ourselves with our dreams, which will enable us to acknowledge them while they are taking place. If we remember our dreams, we can immediately start with two simple techniques to foster lucid dreams.

One of them would be to create a reality check habit. This means to research the environment and determine whether we are awake or dreaming; to ask ourselves many times a day: "Will I be dreaming?" Then, we need to verify the stability of the present reality by reading some words, looking far forward and looking backwards while we try to modify all of it.

The instability of dreams is the easiest hint that helps us distinguish between reality and the dream. If the words change, this means we are inside the dream. Taking naps is one of the ways we can gradually increase the opportunities to have lucid dreams. We need to sleep in REM (Rapid Eye Movement), and focus the intention to acknowledge we are dreaming during nap time. Initially, there can be certain difficulty to rest within the dream after lucidity is attained.

This obstacle leads many people to disregard the value of lucid dreaming, as they have experienced only the grasp of knowledge that they are dreaming, followed by an immediate nudge.

Some simple techniques may help us to overcome this problem.

The first step is to create serenity while dreaming.

The lucid dream itself excites, but expressing this excitement may awaken you.

It is important then to suppress the thrill that produces this situation and direct our attention again to the dream.

The second step is that if the dream shows signs of ending, such as fading, loss of clarity or depth of the imagery, spinning may help the dream to turn back.

Even though we think we are awake, we can be surprised by finding out that we are still dreaming.

Lucid or conscious dreaming also helps us guide our dreams in satisfactory directions, enjoy fantastic adventures and overcome nightmares.

They may also be valuable tools to succeed in our awaken lives.

The third step is meditation.

The simple act of meditating focuses our mind in our inner world where dreams emerge from, showing us what we would like to achieve.

People that regularly practice some kind of meditation

tend to experience more lucid dreams.

The type of meditation is not as important as its regular practice.

Those who are lucid dreamers may deliberately use the natural potential of creativity to solve problems, as well as a source of artistic inspiration, enthusiasm and illumination.

Professionals, athletes, leaders or presenters may prepare, practice and polish their animated performances while they are sleeping.

The lucid dream may be specifically used to enhance their lives. It is also possible that the states of consciousness originated during those states or during lucid dreaming result in an increase in our telepathic ability.

José Ingenieros said, "An ideal is faith in the possibility of perfection".

Having a dream is to place yourself in the road of life because life becomes meaningful only when there are dreams to undertake, and in this endeavor lies the purpose of being and living.

Having a dream means being convinced that life has planted in each of us the necessary potential to make our dreams real since we humans are the reflection of our imagination.

Yesterday I was by chance speaking with my friend Javier, who loves Elizabeth passionately, and has patiently awaited her for many years with the unyielding conviction of realizing this dream of love. He told me a transcendental phrase: "Dreams are not for sale". This thought filled me with fervor.

"I have a dream" is the popular name of the most famous and powerful speech of Martin Luther King Jr., when he eloquently spoke about his wish for a future where people of the white and black race could live together in harmony and as equals.

This speech, pronounced on the steps of Lincoln Memorial Center in Washington during the march for jobs and freedom, was a defining moment in the movement for the civil rights in the United States. It is frequently seen as one of the best lectures in history, and occupies the first place among the dissertations of the twentieth century, according to rhetoric experts.

President Barack Obama himself used the same words in his political campaign, thus imbuing American people with faith and hope.

Having a dream carries us from the illusion level to the faith level and in the same moment, the idea of making it possible.

"Faith" - in the words of Saint Thomas Aquinas- "is an act of the intellect, which adheres to the Divine Truth at the command of the will inspired by the grace of God". Faith is not contrary to reason.

Believing does not mean abdication of reason. Faith is not contrary to science either, because one truth cannot contradict another truth.

Truth comes from only one source which can not contradict itself.

Realities are sacred and sacred realities come from the same divine source, which is God.

Saint Augustine asserts how the relation between faith and reason must be: "I believe in order to understand and I understand in order to believe. I believe in order to be and to create."

Undoubtedly, faith plays a major role in achieving our goals, replenishing us with hope and inspiring us to accomplish them.

It is the driving force which leads our steps towards the attainment of our possible ideal.

William C. Stone remarked: "Whatever the mind of man can conceive, it can achieve."

Only what man *believes,* can he create.

Most of us have resigned many of our passions and dreams. We have ceased to believe in ourselves, to believe in that we have learnt from others and that what others believe it must be good for us.

This is an invitation to take up those forgotten dreams piled in the trunk of doubt and place them on the shelf of faith.

Shaping our future is part of human behavior. We have this ability and this right which makes us free citizens.

We cannot achieve joy without the freedom of being. If we want our dreams to come true, we need to shape our destinies and apply a vision of what we seek composed by multidimensional images which can give us a road map to the chosen direction.

The GPS may help us arrive at the final objective.

And which is the final scheme? The one that each of us chose individually for our best evolution in this level of consciousness.

We always have the freedom to choose our destiny, as well as the various paths and means to arrive there.

What really matters is to convert our trip in something ideal and possible, and enjoy every second of the journey in this terrestrial exploration.

While living in the state of Florida I was able to experience the flow of nature in the midst of a tropical hurricane's force. I learnt something there that changed my point of view as regards of life itself.

In the past, I used to think that the deeper the roots of a tree were, the stronger the resistance it would exhibit to the extremely high winds with which the vicissitudes of life test us.

Yet, and to my great surprise, with the passage of hurricane Wilma in October 2005, I found that most old trees bearing heavy deep roots, were lying on the ground, while the slender palm trees remained in their upright position.

Palm trees show great endurance against the most sweeping winds, for their "flexible" nature. Adapting to these "changes" in a timely manner enables them to stand still without collapsing.

This new approach for me shed some light also on how to be flexible and adapt to the situations that may arise on our life path,-feeling un–attached and, "moving" - fast without resistance towards the unexpected.

I must insist that nature holds the necessary educational "keys" to understand our cosmology and is burdened with answers to our questions.

The journey of a thousand miles starts with a single step. And this first step is our "will" to walk and enjoy the journey with love and peace in our souls.

Feeling the "heartbeat" of the earth, vibrating in unison through our senses, with the certainty of knowing there is a light inside each of us that shines like a sun leading our steps.

This being-consciousness-light empowers us to jump into the heavenly void with the wings of our souls.

Light is always there, but nobody except you can open your eyes to see it.

The Bible says in Proverbs 13:9: "The light of the righteous is joyful."

Walk with happiness within your heart knowing **you are the owner of your dreams and your destiny.**

Turn on your light!

When this light is fully lit inside you, nothing or nobody will separate you from your *ideal possibility.*

The light that illuminates us every day and makes us shudder with joy and excitement when we come across a four-leaf clover.

Bibliography

Bible. Latin-American Pastoral Edition. 1989.

Bloch Arthur. *Murphy's Laws*. 2001.

Bucay Jorge. *Let Me Tell You a Story*. 2005.

Byrne Rhonda. *The Secret*. 2006.

Castaneda Carlos. *Tales of Power*. 2002.

Chopra Deepak. *The Way of the Wizard*. 1995.

Cooper Robert K. *The Other 90%*.

Dalai Lama. *The Art of Happiness*. 2004.

Darwin Charles. *The Origin of the Species*. 2003.

Emoto Masaru. *Messages from the Water*. 2005.

Frankl Viktor. *Man Search for Meaning*. 2006.

Galvis Rams Hortensia. *Acts of Love*. 2005.

Gardner Howard E. *Multiple Intelligence*.

Goleman Daniel. *Emotional Intelligence*. Revision by John D Mayer & Peter Salovey. 2004.

González Lázaro. *The Secret of the Emerald Table*. 2008.

Kornfield Jack. *Living Dharma*. 1995.

LaBerge Stephen. *Dreaming and Consciousness.* Conferene Tucson, Arizona, on April 8, 1996.

Martinez José B. *The Wheel.*

Martinez Meléndez Cristina & Polo Viamontes Margarita, Catalina Pichardo. *That's Us.*

Nervo Amado. *Poetic Anthology.*

Osho. *Inteligence: The Creative Response to Now.* 2004.

Schwartz David. *The Magic of Thinking Big.* 1959

Shakespeare William. *Hamlet.*

St. Augustine. *Confessions.* Prana Publishers. 2006.

Wilde Oscar. *The Fisherman and his Soul.* 1912.

Zweig Connie & Abrams Jeremiah. *Meeting the Shadow*

The Author

Claudia Zamora was born on May 11th 1966 in Buenos Aires, Argentina. She is a Certified Life Coach NLP communications specialist and facilitator of various spiritual practices. She is also author of several dynamics in the development of new educational alternatives and special consultant in teacher training programs and applied creativity. Throughout the years, Claudia has used her natural gifts of empathy and intuition to give support to organizational groups, facilitating implementation methods of efficient structures. She is renowned for her ability to translate the findings of religions throughout the world into techniques that are usable by common people in everyday life.

Claudia has also helped entrepreneurs in the process of passing from vision to manifestation, thus creating axial businesses and organizations which promote the right use of their creative potential, gifts and talents. She is currently living her ideal with her family in beautiful North Carolina.

Contact Claudia at
www.claudiazamora.net